13 Day Better Baseball Swing

THE KINETIC CHAIN

Nathan Bolin

Book Cover by Nathan Bolin

Illustrations by Nathan Bolin

1st edition 2023

Library of Congress Control Number: 2023902911

ISBN: 979-8-9877752-1-9

CONTENTS

What is the 13 Day Better Baseball Swing Program?

The 13 Day Better Baseball Swing program is a complete, start to finish, hitting plan designed to help players improve their baseball swing mechanics and power. It is written in a way that any player, parent, or coach can understand and apply at any level of baseball.

The program is structured in such a way that it is divided into 13 days, each day focusing on a specific topic related to hitting, in order of The Kinetic Chain.

One of the main focuses of the program is the concept of The Kinetic Chain, which is the sequence of movements that occur in the body during a baseball swing. The program teaches players how to use the kinetic chain to generate power and control in a swing.

The program includes 35 different drills that are tailored to help players increase bat speed, develop power, improve coordination, and boost overall performance at the plate.

The program covers a wide range of topics including how to properly grip a bat, knob position and control, loading the hands and rear shoulder, contact position, bat vertical angle at impact, and extension in a baseball swing. It also covers the path of the rear arm, how to release the barrel, and discusses bat drag vs bat lag.

An important aspect of the program is the concept of bat lag. Bat lag is the whip effect created in a swing when the barrel travels behind the hands and is how crazy bat speeds are generated. Bat drag is a common issue in youth baseball where the hitter fails to achieve bat lag due to an incorrect path of the rear arm and elbow.

You will learn about the importance of loading properly, maintaining dynamic balance throughout a swing, when front heel plant occurs, and the importance of a stiff front leg and axis of rotation.

A unique idea that is used within the writing is the use of "catch phrases". You will learn how to utilize catch phrases as instructions to say a lot with a little. A player will understand the reminder when they hear the catch phrase, which is useful during drills, batting practice, and live at-bats.

Overall, the 13 Day Better Baseball Swing program is a comprehensive training program that covers a wide range of topics to help players improve their hitting mechanics. It is a great tool for parents and coaches to improve their instruction and for players of all ages and skill levels looking to improve their swing and take their game to the next level.

Goals and Objectives

Objectives of the Training

1. Provide a complete, start to finish, hitting plan that can be used by coaches, parents, and players at any level of baseball

2. Teach players what it feels like to swing with proper mechanics, balance, control, energy, and power

3. Keep the training plan focused, precise, and achievable

4. Write in a way that any parent or coach can understand, learn, and apply to a player or a team

Parents, Coaches, and Players Goals

1. Improve a player's swing mechanics, increase bat speed, develop power, enhance knowledge, improve coordination, and boost overall performance at the plate.

2. Learn strategies to teach proper batting mechanics through isolation drills. Acquire an understanding of the biomechanics of a swing and the Kinetic Chain.

3. Learn how to identify which stages of a swing need refinement and how to focus on refining those movements.

4. Learn how to utilize catch phrases as instructions to say a lot with a little.

    a) The player will understand the reminder when they hear the catch phrase, which is useful during drills, batting practice, and live at-bats.

    b) See catchphrases in action during their corresponding day of training.

What is The Kinematic Chain?

A German engineer named Franz Reuleaux is credited with the discovery of the concept of the kinematic chain in mechanical systems in 1875. He is considered the father of kinematics, the branch of mechanics that deals with the motion of objects without considering the forces that cause the motion. It deals with the position, velocity, and acceleration of an object over time.

Reuleaux's main contribution to the field of kinematics was the introduction of the concept of the kinematic chain, which he used to describe the movement of interconnected mechanical parts in machinery, such as gears and levers. He observed that these mechanical parts work together in a coordinated and interconnected manner during movement and that this coordination is critical for efficient and effective movement. He proposed that by analyzing the movement of each part of the kinematic chain, it is possible to understand the overall movement of the machine and how it works.

Reuleaux's work laid the foundation for the study of kinematics and his concept of the kinematic chain is still widely used in the field of robotics and mechanical engineering to analyze and design machines and mechanisms. His work also served as an inspiration for researchers in the field of biomechanics and kinesiology, who later adapted the concept of the kinematic chain into the study of human movement, calling it the "kinetic" chain.

What is The Kinetic Chain in Human Movement?

The concept of the kinetic chain in human movement was first introduced by Arthur Steindler, a physical therapist and kinesiologist in the early 1900s. He applied the mechanical principles of the kinematic chain to the study of human movement and developed the concept of the kinetic chain to describe sequences of movements in humans. Steindler published extensively on the subject, and his work laid the foundation for the development of the concept of the kinetic chain in human movement and physical therapy.

The kinetic chain, different from the kinematic chain, does consider the forces that cause the motion. It accounts for the body's movement and how each joint and muscle work together to generate and transfer power during a specific movement. It takes into consideration the body's muscle and skeletal systems, as well as the external forces acting on the body.

Steindler observed that different body parts work together in a coordinated and interconnected manner during movement and that this coordination is critical for efficient and effective movement. He proposed that by assessing and treating the entire kinetic chain, rather than just the site of pain or injury, healthcare professionals could more effectively address the underlying cause of musculoskeletal injuries and improve patient outcomes.

The concept of the kinetic chain was later expanded upon by other physical therapists and researchers in the field of kinesiology and biomechanics. They observed that the kinetic chain starts with the feet and legs, the foundation for movement, and then moves through the core and into the upper body, including the shoulders and arms.

Since then, the concept of the kinetic chain has been widely adopted in the fields of physical therapy, sports medicine, and athletic training. It has been applied to the assessment, treatment, and prevention of musculoskeletal injuries, as well as to the improvement of athletic performance.

Simple acts such as squatting down to pick something up involve over 200 bones and 650 muscles in the human body. This idea that one movement has the ability to affect multiple muscles, tendons, ligaments, and joints at one time is the foundation of understanding the kinetic chain.

The discovery of the kinetic chain in human movement by Arthur Steindler has revolutionized the way we think about human movement and modern-day athletic training. The kinetic chain highlights the interdependence and interconnection of different body segments, and how dysfunction or imbalances in one segment can influence the entire body movement.

What is The Kinetic Chain in a Baseball Swing?

The kinetic chain in a baseball swing refers to the sequential movement of different body parts that work together to generate power and speed in the swing. The kinetic chain starts with the lower body, including the legs and hips, and then moves through the core and into the upper body, including the shoulders and arms.

The lower body plays a critical role in the kinetic chain by providing the foundation for the swing and the point at which power is generated through the transfer of energy. The rear knee, legs, and hips initiate the swing by shifting weight from the back foot to the front foot, which creates torque in the core and sets the upper body in motion. This torque is then transferred through the core and into the shoulders and arms, where it is used to generate the power needed to hit bombs.

The core is also an important link in the kinetic chain, as it helps to stabilize the body and transfer energy from the lower body to the upper body. A strong core allows the upper body to rotate with greater speed and efficiency, which in turn helps to generate more power in the swing.

The upper body, including the shoulders and arms, lags slightly behind the bottom half and completes the kinetic chain. The shoulders and arms rotate around the core, using the energy generated by the lower body and core to create power and speed in the swing.

The kinetic chain in a baseball swing is a complex and coordinated sequence of movements that work together. By understanding the role of each body part in the kinetic chain, players can improve their swing mechanics and hit the ball with more power and accuracy.

The Order of The Kinetic Chain in a Baseball Swing

1. **Stance**
   a. Grip on the Bat
   b. Lower Half: Toes, Knees
   c. Hand Position
2. **Load**
   a. Legs, Hands & Shoulder
3. **Stride**
   a. Dynamic Balance : Head over Sternum over Belly Button
   b. Walk Away From Hands
4. **Hips**
   a. Ground-Up Swing : Load, Stride, Hips
   b. Center of Axis Rotation on Stiff Front Leg
   c. Back Knee Rotation, Toe Drag, No Bug Smashing
5. **Hands**
   a. Hand Path and Hands Inside the Ball
   b. Bat Lag, not Bat Drag
   c. Short to Long Swing
6. **Contact**
   a. Palm Up, Palm Down
   b. Bat Vertical Angle at Impact
   c. Stay Behind the Ball
7. **Extension**
   a. Push Through Contact Before Rolling Over
8. **Follow Through**
   a. Chin From Shoulder to Shoulder / Eyes Stay at Contact
   b. Finish Over Top of Front Shoulder

Training Plan

Days 1-3 : Stance, Load, Stride

Day 1 : Stance, Grip on the Bat and Loading the Legs

Day 2 : Loading the Hands

Day 3 : Walk Away from the Hands

Days 4-6 : Launch Position & Hip Explosion

Day 4: Striding into Launch Position

Day 5 : Leading Your Swing with Your Hips

Day 6 : Weight Transfer - Rear Loaded Weight to the Front Leg

Days 7-9 : Controlling the Top Half

Day 7 : Path of The Rear Arm, Bat Drag Vs Lag, and Barrel Release

Day 8 : Keeping the Front Shoulder Closed

Day 9 : Hand Path and Hands Inside the Ball

Days 10-13 : Contact and Finishing the Swing

Day 10 : Contact Position and Bat Vertical Angle at Impact

Day 11 : Load & Stride, Slot, Contact - Build the muscle memory

Day 12 : Extension & Follow Through

Day 13 : Bringing It All Together

The Theory of Catch Phrases

If the nickname of the game that you are playing is "The Thinking Man's Game", I'd try hard to facilitate players being able to think. I wouldn't and don't, obstruct a player's thought process with constant instruction.

Catch Phrases let you give meaningful direction to the hitter while allowing time for him to think on his own. One that I used for a while to remind my son to use powerful rotational force was "Strong Hips". Since we had performed drills that were related to this, he understood what this meant. I have a clip of a homerun where before the at bat, the only words that I say to him are: "Track the Ball, See the Contact … Strong Hips … Lift It" https://youtu.be/m5LDycQJzzs?t=122

With those phrases, I reminded him to start with and keep both eyes on the pitcher by not rolling the front shoulder too much during load, keep his head at contact, lead his swing with a strong hip explosion, get to extension without rolling his wrists over, and finish his swing over the top of his shoulder.

It could have been something about his hand positioning during load, not pulling his front shoulder, being squared in his stance, having fast hands, being on time, staying on top of the ball, or getting on plane early. However, working with him, I knew where the focus should be and was able to direct his mindset and approach with a few keywords, or "Catch Phrases".

The player MUST have the opportunity to mentally focus and self-reflect as an individual during an at bat. For example, realizing that you loaded late, pulled your front side, or did not keep your head at contact on the last swing. The player should be thinking about how to adjust on the next swing and more so, thinking about the count, pitch scenario, and the situation of the game.

When a player is on deck or steps out of the box and takes a couple of practice swings, he is practicing what it feels like to make whatever adjustment he feels is required. He is not just swinging to get his body loose. He is practicing the mechanics of a proper swing and thinking about his approach to the situation that he will face during his at-bat. He is using the knowledge from training to prepare for performing a 'good swing'.

Coaches and parents that over communicate with a player distract from this mental approach and ability to self-reflect, adjust, and prepare for the next swing with an updated approach. Catch phrases are hints to the player on where his train of thought should be and what adjustments he should be thinking about for his next swing.

The ability for a player to make adjustments and understand how to adjust is built through repeated verbal and physical training. Great athletes are not created during live gameplay.

List of Catch Phrases

CATCH PHRASE: FINGERS
REMINDS TO: Check that the top hand index and middle fingers form a V towards the back shoulder. Line up the knocking knuckles and check that the bat handle is being gripped by the fingers, not the palms.

CATCH PHRASE: TOES AND KNEES
REMINDS TO: Point toes straight ahead and start with BOTH knees slightly bent. Keep hips closed and weight on the inside of the back foot.

CATCH PHRASE: FLASHLIGHT (or KNOB CONTROL)
REMINDS TO: Control the path of the knob before and after load. Have the knob of the bat pointed near the catcher's glove when loaded.

CATCH PHRASE: WALK AWAY
REMINDS TO: Create separation between the hands and stride foot. Walk away from the hands.

CATCH PHRASE: SOFT STEP, STAY STRONG
REMINDS TO: Land softly on the ball of the stride foot. Stay in alignment and keep the core strong throughout the stride. Have Dynamic Balance.

CATCH PHRASE: STRONG HIPS
REMINDS TO: Start the swing with a strong hip explosion to create rotational force. Create weight transfer by turning and driving the rear knee forward.

CATCH PHRASE: RELEASE
REMINDS TO: Feel the bat lag (slotted) position and achieve barrel release on the swing.

CATCH PHRASE: SHORT TO LONG
REMINDS TO: Get the barrel into the strike zone with the shortest path and keep the barrel through the strike zone as long as possible.

CATCH PHRASE: LIFT IT
REMINDS TO: Continue pushing through contact without rolling the wrists over. Feel extension towards center field and finish over the front shoulder.

What equipment do you need?

1. **Batting Tee:** I highly suggest a rolled rubber top. A player receives better feedback on contact with the baseball.
   https://www.tannertees.com/tanner-tee-the-original

2. **Hitting Net:** I've used the PowerNet 7 x7 ft for over 4 years without issue.
   https://www.amazon.com/gp/product/B00NG1ECBS

3. **Hitting Lane or Open Field:** There are several soft-toss drills that require a hitting lane or open field.

4. **(Optional) Half Bat:** Practice bat with a flat barrel
   https://www.halfbat.com/collections/all

5. **(Optional) Anywhere Balls:** Soft foam baseballs for use with a half bat or training "anywhere".
   https://www.amazon.com/gp/product/B00GWYK28I

List of Drills

ID	Day	Drill	Drill Name
1	1	1	GRIP, STANCE, AND LOAD REVIEW
2	1	2	GRIP, STANCE, AND LOAD CHECKPOINTS
3	2	1	REAR SHOULDER PINCH
4	2	2	LASER KNOB
5	2	3	SIMULATED LASER KNOB TEE
6	3	1	LOAD CHECK STRIDE CHECK HIT
7	3	2	TWO STEP WALK UP
8	4	1	FRONT FOOT BALL STEP CHECK
9	4	2	FRONT FOOT BALL STEP TEE
10	4	3	STRIDE BOX
11	5	1	STANCE, LOAD, STRIDE, HIP SEQUENCE CHECK
12	5	2	REAR ELBOW GLOVE THROW
13	5	3	BAT LAG TO EXTENSION TEE
14	5	4	BAT LAG TO EXTENSION FRONT TOSS
15	6	1	HIP EXPLOSION ISOLATION
16	6	2	THE GRIFFEY
17	6	3	REAR KNEE FOLLOW THROUGH
18	6	4	REAR NET
19	7	1	REAR ARM UNDERHAND CATCH
20	7	2	HIGH INSIDE REAR ARM PULL

21	7	3	FAST ATTACK FROM LOADED, STOP AT EXTENSION
22	8	1	SITTING BUCKET ONE ARM HIGH TEE
23	8	2	STANDING ONE ARM HIGH TEE
24	8	3	BACK SIDE SINGLE HAND NET HOLD
25	8	4	CROSS TOSS OUTSIDE
26	8	5	SITTING BUCKET TWO HAND HIGH TEE
27	9	1	KNOB TEE
28	9	2	SWING INSIDE THE NET
29	9	3	SWING INSIDE THE NET TEE
30	9	4	DEEP OPPO TACO
31	9	5	FRONT ARM FRISBEE
32	10	1	FOUR POINT CHECK (LOAD, STRIDE, SLOT, CONTACT) TEE
33	11	1	LOAD & STRIDE, SLOT, HIT
34	11	2	FRONT TOSS FAKE OUT
35	11	3	LINE DRIVE PRO
36	12	1	TOP HAND UPSIDE-DOWN
37	12	2	FLAT PALM TOP HAND
38	12	3	SWING TO CONTACT, RESET AND HOLD FINISH
39	13	1	QUIZ ON CATCH PHRASES AND CHECKPOINTS
40	13	2	FINISH LINE

About the Author

Over the past 10 years, I have gained extensive experience in coaching and developing players of all ages, ranging from 3 to 17. Through this experience, I have honed my skills in identifying and implementing effective strategies for quickly improving hitting mechanics, resulting in an enhanced performance at the plate. My knowledge of hitting mechanics has been constantly expanding through my ongoing studies and research, and I have learned how to effectively apply these mechanics to players of all ages.

While new findings and technology are continually emerging to assist athletes in their training, hitting is still hitting. By watching some of the best MLB players, you will notice that they share similar biomechanics and "steps" in their swings.

I developed my approach by breaking down the biomechanics of hitting in a way that can be easily taught, using it to help my 7-year-old son who had major issues with bat drag. The results were impressive. The following summer he hit 5 out of the park home runs with distances around 180 feet and won the USSSA Kentucky State Showcase Homerun Derby the year after. As an 11-year-old in 2022, he had 10 home runs playing AAA/Open with distances up to 270 ft., with alloy.

While I may not be an MLB player, I have a strong background in baseball. I received a full ride to college on academic and baseball scholarships as a third baseman and pitcher. I am 38 years old and actively play shortstop, pitch, and bat in the top 4 in a competitive 18+ men's league (Kentuckiana Baseball Association). My team, the Kentuckiana Redbirds, was the 2022 league runner-up and won the 2022 Rocket City Classic tournament in Huntsville, Alabama. I have coached teams to countless championships.

By applying the principles outlined in this document, my 11-year-old son was able to achieve impressive results during the 2022 travel season. He finished the season with a .627 batting average, 1.1173 SLG, 1.882 OPS, and a .708 on-base percentage over the course of 96 plate appearances. Additionally, my 16-year-old sophomore was able to finish his high school varsity season with a .358 batting average and a .506 on-base percentage over the course of 87 plate appearances.

DAYS 1-3 : STANCE, LOAD, STRIDE

DAY 1: Stance, Grip on the Bat and Loading the Legs

Stance

A good batting stance is essential for a successful at-bat. It sets the foundation for the swing and helps the batter achieve the proper mechanics and body position to make contact with the ball. A proper stance allows the batter to be balanced, centered, and ready to generate power in the swing. It helps the batter to keep their weight back and maintain proper alignment of their body, which helps to maintain control of the swing and make better contact with the ball. A good stance also allows the batter to be in a better position to track the pitch and adjust as necessary.

Stance, also known as **Pre-Load**, is the starting position for a batter before they initiate their swing. A proper stance includes toes pointing straight ahead, with the option to have them slightly closed. The stance should be slightly open, with the rear foot being slightly closer to the plate. The knees should be bent, with no straight or stiff legs. The feet should be wider than the shoulders and the hands should be in front of the rear shoulder. The bat should be over the shoulder at nearly a 45-degree angle and should be behind the helmet. The top half of the body should be slightly over the plate, not straight up and down. The front shoulder should be slightly rolled with the rear eye still on the pitcher. The hitter should have the jersey number on his back slightly showing to the pitcher.

For more advanced players, the first couple of days are going to seem basic. However, it's important that players at all levels are reminded of proper swing mechanics. When you understand the steps in a swing and the nuances in each of those steps, you develop the ability to self-adjust and make corrections from one swing to another. You can recall certain drills and key movements that can be used for adjusting your swing.

Grip on the Bat

One of the key elements to a proper grip is to ensure that your knuckles are lined up correctly. This is known as the **Knocking Knuckles** grip. This means that the knuckles of your bottom hand should be lined up with the knuckles of your top hand when gripping the bat. This helps to ensure that the bat is held in the correct position, which can help to improve the player's swing and overall performance.

A simple way to get the hands into a good starting position in the stance is to simply rest the bat grip on the rear shoulder and then slightly raise it off the shoulder, pointing the bat knob at the ground near the back of the plate.

KNOCKING KNUCKLES GRIP

There are a few ways to check for a proper grip on a baseball bat:

The "V" Check: One way to check for a proper grip is to look at the position of the hands on the bat. The player should form a "V" shape, or a "peace sign", with the index and middle fingers of their top hand extended. The V should point towards the player's back shoulder. This ensures that the fingers are properly wrapped around the handle, allowing for more control and power in the swing.

The Knuckle Check: Another way to check for a proper grip is to make sure that the knuckles on the top hand are lined up with the knuckles on the bottom hand. This is known as "lining up the knocking knuckles" and it helps to ensure that the bat is held in the correct position.

The Index Check: When a hitter straightens out both index fingers while in his stance, both fingers should be pointing upwards towards the sky, though not completely straight up. This is the easiest way to quickly identify players with over grip.

The Wrist Check: When gripping the bat, the player should ensure that their wrists are in a neutral position, neither too flexed nor too extended, this will allow for better control of the bat during the swing.

The Swing Check: The best way to check for proper grip is to take swings and have a coach or partner observe your swing, they can give feedback on any adjustments that need to be made to your grip.

It's important to note that a proper grip can vary from player to player, and it's important that each player finds the grip that works best for them. However, having a correct grip is important as it helps control the bat during the swing. It's essential to experiment with different grips and find the one that feels most comfortable and generates the most power and control.

CATCH PHRASE: FINGERS
REMINDS TO: Check that the top hand index and middle fingers form a V towards the back shoulder. Line up the knocking knuckles and check that the bat handle is being gripped by the fingers, not the palms.

Loading the Legs

Loading the legs in a baseball swing is the process of preparing the lower body for the swing. This includes positioning the legs and hips in a way that allows for maximum power and control during the swing.

Proper loading of the legs starts with the stance. A proper stance will have the player's weight evenly distributed on both legs, with the legs slightly bent. This allows the player to generate power from their legs and hips during the swing. As the pitcher prepares to release the ball, the batter should then begin to shift their weight to the back leg, this is called loading the leg. This shift in weight is used to generate power in the swing.

Another important aspect of loading the legs is the timing of it. The weight shift should occur at the right moment, ideally just before the pitcher releases the ball. This allows the player to generate maximum power from the legs and hips. Timing is key, if the weight shift is done too soon, it could result in the player being out of balance and off-timing in the swing.

In addition, the player should also engage the glutes and core muscles while loading the legs. This helps to maintain stability and balance throughout the swing. Practicing loading the legs through different drills, such as stride drills, can help players develop proper timing mechanics in their swings. The following checklists highlight the key points to look for as a guide for quick checks.

One key point to note is the position of the hands. They should be in front of the rear shoulder with the knob of the bat pointing towards the ground. Before loading, the hitter should be in a strong and balanced athletic position.

By following these steps, players can ensure that they are loading properly and setting themselves up for a successful swing.

Day 1 DRILL #1
GRIP, STANCE, AND LOAD REVIEW
Review the following CHECKPOINTS and quiz the player on positioning.

<u>CHECKPOINTS:</u>

1. **Stance** (Pre-Load)
    1. Toes point straight ahead (can be more closed)
    2. Stance is slightly open, rear foot is slightly closer to the plate
    3. Knees are BENT, no straight or stiff legs
    4. Feet are wider than shoulders
    5. Hands in front of rear shoulder
    6. Bat is over the shoulder at nearly a 45-degree angle
    7. Bat is behind the helmet
    8. Top half is slightly over the plate, not straight up and down
2. **Load**
    1. Weight of the back foot is on the inside, NOT outside, of the rear foot and is ready to launch towards the pitched ball.
    2. Front shoulder is slightly rolled with both eyes able to see the pitcher. Don't roll your front shoulder too much as you load and take away your rear eye from seeing the ball.
    3. Knees and hips pinch together - almost as if a ball is being squeezed between the knees. ("Closed hips")
    4. Back knee and front knee stay bent throughout load

Day 1 DRILL #2
GRIP, STANCE, AND LOAD CHECKPOINTS

3 sets of 5 reps

Get into a proper stance and say load. Say each of the checkpoints out loud while loaded and hit a ball off a tee from this position. When performing tee drills, make sure that contact is occurring in front of the front leg

<u>CHECKPOINTS</u>:

1. Knees bent
2. Weight on inside of back foot
3. Hands back, in front of shoulder
4. Knob at catcher
5. Grip *(Stick index fingers out, should point upwards)*
6. Both eyes on pitcher

CATCH PHRASE: TOES AND KNEES
REMINDS TO: Point toes straight ahead and start with BOTH knees slightly bent. Keep hips closed and weight on the inside of the back foot.

DAY 2: Loading the Hands

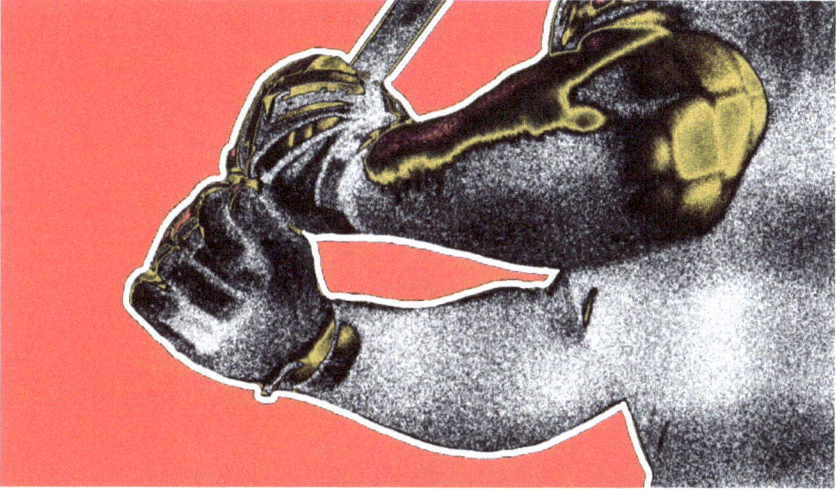

Loading the hands in a baseball swing is the process of moving the hands and wrists into the proper position before starting the swing. This movement helps to create a compact and efficient swing, as it allows the hands to be in the correct position to generate power and control. A proper load of the hands is essential for a powerful and accurate swing.

One key aspect of loading the hands is keeping them close to the body, specifically in front of the rear shoulder. Having the hands in this position allows for the hitter to transition into the "slot position" which will be discussed in detail in later training.

In addition to keeping the hands close to the body, the hands should be in a position where they can rotate around the axis of the bat. This rotation helps to create the power and control needed for a successful swing. Players should practice loading the hands in their swing by keeping their hands close to the body and rotating them around the axis of the bat; This can be done by using different drills such as laser knob drills, or by using a weight on the end of the bat to practice the motion. It's important to note that a proper load of the hands can vary from player to player, and each player must find the load the load that works best for them. However, having a correct load can help with the control and power of the swing.

I do not emphasize pushing the hands back because I have seen it result in bad mechanics where players end up barring out the front arm. We will be walking away from the hands more so and creating separation between the hands and front foot during the stride.

A key movement included with loading the hands is loading the rear shoulder. This controls the movement which points the knob towards the catcher. Focus on this rear shoulder "rolling in" movement when loading. One way to describe this motion is while in your stance, the rear hand moves as if it is very slightly pouring out a coffee mug inward in the direction of the rear shoulder or chest. Observe the illustration above and notice that if the player was holding a coffee mug in the top hand, it would be pouring out as described.

In a proper batting stance, the hitter should position their body in such a way that their jersey number is somewhat visible to the pitcher, while also keeping their hands hidden from the pitcher's view. This technique is known as **Hiding Your Hands**. This can help to create a more efficient and powerful swing by keeping the hands in the right position for optimal movement.

It's important to note that loading the hands is a personal thing and can vary from player to player, and each player must find the load that works best for them. Having a correct load can help with the control and timing of the swing.

REPEAT Day 1 DRILL #2
STANCE AND LOAD CHECKPOINTS
2 sets of 5 reps

Day 2 DRILL #1
REAR SHOULDER PINCH
3 sets of 5 reps
Perform the first set of 5 reps without a bat, using a two-hand grip on your invisible bat. From a normal resting stance, slightly roll the rear shoulder inwards as if you are pouring out a coffee mug towards your chest. This moves the hands back and points the knob at the catcher. This is a SMALL movement. Control the path of the knob. The position should be very similar to your position if you were preparing to throw a strong punch.

CHECKPOINTS:

1. Toes pointed straight ahead, and knees are bent

2. Position of the hands:
    1. Hands are in front of rear shoulder from a side view
    2. Hands are in front of toe line from top-down view
    3. Wrists are angled, not flat with the forearms.
    4. **We are NOT pushing the hands back**
3. Knob of bat points at or near catcher's glove
4. Hitter is hiding hands from the pitcher
5. **Slight** stretch in leading arm deltoid and lat muscles but NOT barring out the arm

Day 2 DRILL #2
LASER KNOB
3 sets of 5 reps

Rig up a laser pointer or flashlight to the bottom of the bat handle with some tape. Get into a normal stance with the laser pointed toward the ground near the back of the plate. Load slowly and move the laser dot in a straight line away from the back tip of the plate. Once in the loaded position with the laser pointed towards the catcher, move the laser dot back up the straight line that you first made using your wrists only as much as possible and keeping your hands back near the rear shoulder. Once the straight line of the laser dot gets well past the front of the plate, snap to the contact position.

Day 2 DRILL #3
SIMULATED LASER KNOB TEE
3 sets of 8 reps

Remove the laser pointer and perform the same action with a simulated laser pointer on the end of your knob. Load slowly and move the simulated laser dot in a straight line away from the back tip of the plate. Once in the loaded position with the laser pointed towards the catcher, move the laser dot back up the straight line that you first made using only your wrists as much as possible. Once the straight line of the simulated laser dot gets well past the front of the plate, hit the ball off the tee and finish with both arms extended, pointing towards center field

CATCH PHRASE: FLASHLIGHT (or KNOB CONTROL)
REMINDS TO: Control the path of the knob before and after load. Have the knob of the bat pointed near the catcher's glove when loaded.

DAY 3: Walk Away from the Hands

Now that we have a feel for loading properly and understand what a strong stance and pre-load position feels like, let's create some separation between the front leg and the hands. This should be a very smooth motion. Reiterate being relaxed with some rhythm before loading and watch several slow-motion MLB swings for reference. Variance in stance and load does exist but anyone that hits with power creates this separation between the front foot and the hands before hip explosion and launch.

Take a small step to increase your power. Once the ball leaves the pitcher's hand (or the machine), step out slightly with the front foot. Only move the foot a few inches forward and be careful not to come out of alignment or lose tightness in your core as you step. This will increase the power of the swing by adding directional force to the rotational motion of the hips and shoulders. Imagine the hitter has a rubber band attached to the knob of the bat and the other end attached to the stride foot. We want this rubber band to get stretched out and stay stretched when the hips start to rotate.

The movement is called **Walking Away From the Hands** because the hands move away from the body as if the batter is walking away from their hands. This motion helps to create a powerful and efficient swing. The hands move to the slot position as you are walking away from them.

The **Slot Position** in a baseball swing refers to the position of the upper body just before the swing begins. The hands are typically lower with the bat in a vertical position and pointing toward the ground. This position is called the slot because it is like the position a slot machine arm is in when it is ready to be pulled. This position allows the batter to generate power and maintain control of the swing as they begin their motion toward the ball. Additionally, having the hands and bat in the slot position allows for a more direct and efficient path to the ball.

The movement of walking away from the hands can be considered an advanced technique and is often taught to more experienced players. It is important to note that different players may have different techniques for their swing, and it's important for players to find the technique that works best for them.

REPEAT Day 1 DRILL #2
STANCE AND LOAD CHECKPOINTS
1 set of 8 reps

REPEAT Day 2 DRILL #1
REAR SHOULDER LOAD ROLL
2 set of 5 reps

REPEAT Day 2 DRILL #3
SIMULATED LASER KNOB TEE
3 sets of 8 reps

Day 3 DRILL #1
LOAD CHECK STRIDE CHECK HIT
3 sets of 8 reps
Load, check hands, stride, check hands. Say each out loud or in your head during the movements. Briefly pause at each step. Reset and hit one ball off the tee without pausing at each step to complete one rep.

CHECKPOINTS:

1. Hands and top half are the same when loaded and after the stride
2. Feet are about one bat length apart
3. Front knee slightly bent after stride
4. Front shoulder stays slightly lower than rear shoulder
5. From side view, core and upper half stays vertically straight
6. Stride foot is at 30-45 degree when landing
7. Elbows stay separated throughout stance, load, and hip explosion.
8. Core / Belly Button does not travel forwards towards the pitcher

Day 3 DRILL #2
TWO STEP WALK UP

3 sets of 8 reps

Stand Behind the batter's box with your chest facing the pitcher. Take two steps forward, stride foot first, and plant your rear foot into the batter's box on the second step. Have the rear foot turned and facing in the correct direction when it lands. Continue into your stride to hit the ball off the tee. Feel the separation being created between your stride foot and your hands. Feel how your core wants to coil up as you rotate your body into the hitting position.

CATCH PHRASE: WALK AWAY
REMINDS TO: Create separation between the hands and stride foot. Walk away from the hands.

Days 4-6 : Launch Position & Hip Explosion

DAY 4: Striding Into Launch Position

We are still setting ourselves up to start our swing at the ball. This step is crucial in maintaining balance and alignment so that we can rotate on an axis.

Load and stride are instantaneous motions. A hitter typically loads on or just before the pitcher's leg lift. If you are coaching sling-arm machine pitch age, load when the sling-arm operator raises his opposite arm just before throwing the pitch. The timing mechanism to load is the arm being raised since this action is meant to simulate a live pitcher's leg lift.

Once stride is taken, the front foot is at a 30 to 45-degree angle and the knob of the bat is pointed near the catcher's glove. The stride should be short, soft, and slow. The stride is separate from the actual swing.

You do not step **and** hit. You step **to** hit. If you're using the no-step approach, you will need to shift into this position following your load action. With a no-step swing, I encourage the player to pick up and set down the front foot to simulate the stride.

The Launch Position, also referred to as **The Ready to Hit Position**, is the position you're in at the end of your stride just as your front foot touches down. It's important to note this because it controls the timing of your swing.

Many swings in youth baseball go bad right here by failing to get into a good launch position or getting into it too late. If you're not in a good launch position, you are going to struggle to hit the ball consistently. When your front foot touches down, you should be in the following position:

1. The feet are about one bat length apart
    Front Heel Plant will trigger Opposing Rotation of Toes
2. The weight of the front foot is on the ball of the foot, and the heel is slightly up.
    Front Heel Plant will trigger rear knee rotation and hip explosion.
3. Weight is centered or slightly back and hips are still square/closed
4. Upper Half is vertically aligned over the belly button and not tilted.
    Dynamic Balance = Head over Sternum over Belly Button
5. The front shoulder stays closed, and the back shoulder is slightly higher than the front
6. Both eyes are on the pitcher and able to track the ball
7. The hands stay back, and stride creates separation between the hands and the body. "Walk away from your hands."

Being in a good launch position sets up the next movement in the kinetic chain, which is pinching the rear shoulder towards the rear hip or "slotting the rear elbow". This "rear shoulder pinching" movement is a crucial step in the kinetic chain and should develop naturally if following the drills in this training plan. By focusing on the proper launch position and initiating the kinetic chain correctly, a player can optimize their swing mechanics, increase bat speed & power, and improve their overall performance at the plate.

Day 1 DRILL #1
STANCE AND LOAD REVIEW
Review the CHECKPOINTS and quiz the hitter on positioning.

REPEAT Day 3 DRILL #1
LOAD CHECK STRIDE CHECK HIT
2 sets of 5 reps

Day 4 DRILL #1
FRONT FOOT BALL STEP CHECK

2 sets of 5 reps

Place a medicine ball, or basketball, under the front foot while in a batting stance. Feel the activation in the quad, hamstring, and heel. Feel how stable you are. Raise the front foot off the top of the ball and slowly step over it towards the pitcher. Land in a ready-to-hit position on the ball of the front foot. Remember that we are not yet planting the front heel. That will occur with hip rotation.

Day 4 DRILL #2
FRONT FOOT BALL STEP TEE

2 sets of 8 reps

Place a medicine ball, or basketball, under the front foot while in a batting stance. Feel the activation in the quad, hamstring, and heel. Raise the front foot off the top of the ball and step over it towards the pitcher, hitting the ball off the tee.

Day 4 DRILL #3
STRIDE BOX

3 sets of 8 reps

To perform this drill, a small flat box or a square of tape is placed on the ground in front of the batter, representing the ideal stride position. The batter should take their normal stance and focus on striding into the box and keeping dynamic balance. The batter should make sure that their front foot lands within the box or tape and that their weight is distributed evenly between both legs. We are taking a small step and landing softly on the ball of the front foot with a bent knee.

After the first set of 8 reps, or once the batter is comfortable with striding into the box, they can progress to taking swings while focusing on maintaining their launch position. The coach or partner can observe the batter and give feedback on any adjustments that need to be made.

REPEAT Day 3 DRILL #2
TWO STEP WALK UP

3 sets of 5 reps

CATCH PHRASE: SOFT STEP, STAY STRONG
REMINDS TO: Land softly on the ball of the stride foot. Stay in alignment and keep the core strong throughout the stride. Have Dynamic Balance.

DAY 5: Leading Your Swing with Your Hips

Working with hundreds of youth players has taught me that many young players tend to lead a swing with the top half of the body rather than with the hips. They are simply thinking about getting the barrel around which causes them to lead their swings with the top half, leaving the hips trailing in the swing. You can't hit a ball with power if you do not have separation in the top and bottom half of your body in the early stages of your swing. The bottom half leads the swing.

In today's drills, you should start to feel the connection between firing your hips and firing your hands. You should feel your hands and top half resisting the rotational force of your lower body. It is with this lagged whip effect that insane bat speed is created.

Bat Lag refers to the delay in the movement of the bat's barrel behind the hands during the downswing phase of a baseball swing. This is the moment in a swing where the bat is flat and nearly parallel to the ground. During this phase, the lower body's rotational force is transferred into the upper body.

BAT LAG POSITION

An analogy that I use for teaching timing of a swing is to imagine a button underneath the stride foot heel after the hitter has taken his stride and is in the ready-to-hit launch position. Pressing this button down into the ground by performing "Front Heel Plant" is what triggers rear knee rotation and hip explosion.

The **Front Heel Plant** is the point in the swing where the front heel meets the ground and the weight of the body is transferred to the front leg.

One important aspect to consider when discussing the front heel plant is the axis of rotation. The axis of rotation is the point around which the body rotates during the swing. A key component in generating power and control is maintaining a proper axis of rotation throughout the swing. This is achieved by keeping the front leg stiff, which allows the player to generate power from the lower body and transfer it to the upper body.

It's also important to note that having a stiff front leg during the swing helps to maintain the axis of rotation and it's important that players practice keeping the front leg stiff. This can be done through exercises such as lunges or squats that focus on building strength in the legs.

However, it's important to note that a stiff front leg doesn't mean a locked front knee, it means that the front knee should be slightly flexed and ready to move but not locked. This will allow for a better transfer of energy and power during the swing, help to avoid injury, and result in better dynamic balance.

Day 5 DRILL #1
STANCE, LOAD, STRIDE, HIP SEQUENCE CHECK
2 sets of 5 reps

Say each step out loud, or in your head, while moving to each position. Pause in between and check each position. We are NOT moving the hands forward or getting into the slot position. On the word hip, you are opening the hips and rotating your bottom half to feel the separation and stretch in your front deltoid and lat while keeping your hands back. Start to flatten out the bat by turning the knob towards the pitcher on the word hips. Feel the connection between firing your hips and firing your hands. Feel how you can adjust the timing between your hips and hands to create either a short contact swing or a loaded-up power swing.

Day 5 DRILL #2
REAR ELBOW GLOVE THROW
3 sets of 8 reps

Tuck a glove or deflated ball in-between the rear elbow and the hip. Throw it in front of the plate when hitting the ball off a tee. You are not hitting with power, just focusing on the direction of the glove throw up the middle.

Day 5 DRILL #3
BAT LAG TO EXTENSION TEE
3 sets of 8 reps

Start at Bat lag (slotted) position with the rear elbow on the hip and the knob towards the pitcher. The barrel of the bat should be near the rear arm. Hit off the tee and finish in the extension position without rolling the wrists over. The end of the barrel should point towards center field.

Day 5 DRILL #4
BAT LAG TO EXTENSION FRONT TOSS
3 sets of 8 reps

Repeat with front soft toss. 3 sets of 8 reps. Start at Bat lag (slotted) elbow on hip position. Hit and finish in the extension position without rolling the wrists over.

DAY 6: Weight Transfer - Transferring Rear Loaded Weight to the Front Leg

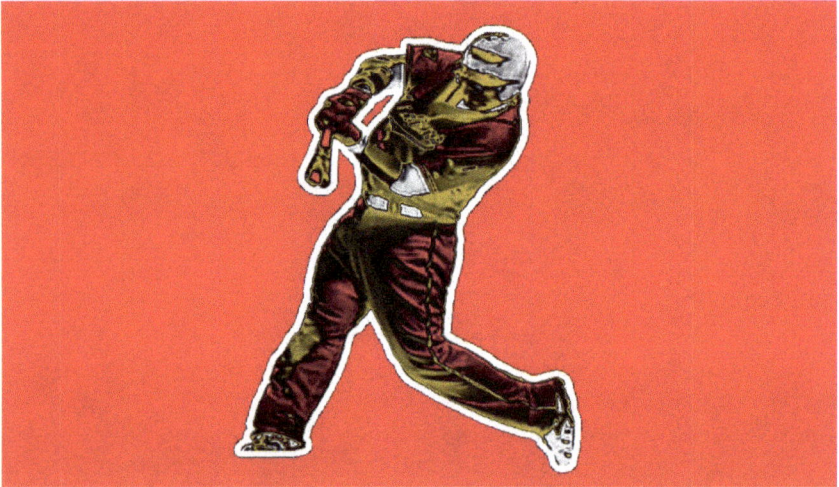

I am a believer that this occurs naturally in many players, so we are not spending too much time on this step in the swing. If we overemphasize this, we can end up with a hitter who has too much weight on the front leg early in the swing resulting in a lunge at the ball motion on a collapsing front side. I am a big proponent of driving your back knee as your hips explode which naturally forces weight to be transferred to the front foot. If the player has learned to get into a good launch position, and actually launches, he is probably doing a decent job of transferring weight to the front leg. With a very aggressive launch, you will even see the rear toe drag. You can see some MLB hitters raising completely off the rear foot at contact. We **ARE NOT** "squashing the bug".

https://www.youtube.com/watch?v=BmZnUEsFnbw
Jose Altuve Slow Motion Swing

Some players have a good response to telling them that the back knee should be in front of the buttocks at contact. This is the meaning that I take away from the common baseball saying, "Sit on One."

Weight transfer also allows the player to generate power and accuracy in their swing. Proper weight transfer begins with the player shifting their weight from their back foot to their front foot during the pre-launch phase of the swing. This shift of weight creates tension in the legs and core, which can be used to generate explosive power when the player starts their swing. By transferring weight in the right way, the player can increase the speed of their bat and create more force to hit the ball farther.

Another important aspect of weight transfer is the distribution of weight throughout the swing. During the stride phase, the player should focus on maintaining a balanced distribution of weight throughout the body, with most of the weight shifting to the front leg. This allows the player to maintain their dynamic balance and stay centered throughout the swing. As the player contacts the ball, they should shift the majority of their weight to their back leg, creating a strong base for the follow-through of the swing. By understanding and executing proper weight transfer, players can improve their swing mechanics and hit the ball with more power and accuracy.

POSITION OF FEET WITH PROPER WEIGHT TRANSFER

Day 6 DRILL #1
HIP EXPLOSION ISOLATION
2 sets of 8 reps
From the loaded position, take a small stride step. When the front heel touches down, explosively rotate the back knee towards the front leg as fast as possible to trigger hip rotation. Enforce the hitter shifting the loaded weight forward toward the pitcher. This movement should cause the rear heel to raise, and even better if we can simulate some rear foot toe drag. The hands and knob should be firing into the slot position immediately after the hips

Day 6 DRILL #2
THE GRIFFEY
3 sets of 8 reps
Get into your batting stance with your feet almost all the way together. Make sure to relax your hands. When taking a step forward, you should naturally create separation between your stride food and hands. When your stride foot lands, make sure that you are in a good ready-to-hit launch position. You want to feel nice and relaxed and use the planting of the stride foot heel as a timing mechanism to fire the hips and start the swing.

Day 6 DRILL #3
REAR KNEE FOLLOW THROUGH
3 sets of 8 reps
From a normal stance and with normal timing, hit a ball off the tee and finish with your rear knee continuing forward and upward. Feel the axis or rotation on a stiffened front leg. Feel opposing rotation in the front side of your body, meaning that you can feel your front leg and front of your core resist the backside rotation from the rear knee and hips. This stabilizes the batter and helps to maintain dynamic balance (head over sternum over belly button).

Day 6 DRILL #4
REAR NET
3 sets of 8 reps
Get into a batting stance with your rear foot about 4-6 inches away from a net or fence behind you. Stride away from the rear net/fence to hit the ball off a tee. The player should be able to swing without hitting the rear net/fence.

REPEAT Day 4 DRILL #3
STRIDE BOX
3 sets of 8 reps

CATCH PHRASE: STRONG HIPS
REMINDS TO: Start the swing with a strong hip explosion to create rotational force. Create weight transfer by turning and driving the rear knee forward.

DAYS 7-9 : CONTROLLING THE TOP HALF

DAY 7: Path of The Rear Arm, Bat Drag Vs Lag, and Barrel Release

The path of the rear arm, bat lag, and barrel release are all important aspects of a proper baseball swing. The path of the rear arm, also known as the back arm, refers to the movement and positioning of the arm on the side of the body. The rear arm plays a critical role in the swing by providing balance and stability. A proper path of the rear arm involves keeping the elbow close to the body and maintaining a relaxed, yet firm grip on the bat.

PROPER SEQUENCE
Stride foot toe lands, stride foot heel plant, rear knee/hip fires, shoulder axis changes, and the rear arm drops into the slot position

In the above animation, observe the precise timing of the stride foot as it lands on the toes, the simultaneous heel plant, the firing of the rear knee and hip, the change in the shoulder axis, and the hands dropping into the slot position. The timing of this sequence is crucial for a powerful and accurate swing, and it is important to focus on replicating this movement during training.

When a hitter leads a swing with the elbow in front of the hips from a side view, this is called bat drag. **Bat Drag** is the primary example of incorrect rear arm path and is the problem that strikes more youth players than any other swing flaw. It refers to a hitter's inability to keep the rear elbow near the body during rotation and results in a failure to create **Bat Lag**, the whip effect in a swing.

BAT DRAG

Bat Drag is identified by the bat's barrel being behind the hands during the downswing. This is caused by the hands and wrists not rotating properly, resulting in the barrel of the bat not getting to the optimal hitting position at the right time. Bat drag can cause a lack of power and accuracy in the swing, as well as increase the likelihood of swinging and missing or hitting the ball much weaker than expected. It can be corrected by focusing on proper hand and wrist rotation during the swing, and by practicing drills that help to improve this aspect of the swing.

Barrel Release is the point in the swing when the hitter begins to rotate the bat toward the ball. The barrel release is a critical aspect of the swing as it allows the hitter to transfer the power and momentum generated during the backswing into the ball. A proper barrel release involves keeping the hands inside of the ball, allowing the barrel to travel on a direct path to the ball, and maintaining a level swing path to achieve a proper bat vertical angle at impact. This results in a more efficient transfer of energy from the body to the bat and results in harder hits. We will discuss the hand path in depth on Day 9.

The BAT LAG TO EXTENSION drills that have been performed are barrel release isolation drills.

The motion of staying behind the ball is impossible if you have bat drag, which I know from working with my son particularly. The drills for today played a big part in showing him what these important motions feel like.

REPEAT Day 2 DRILL #3
SIMULATED LASER KNOB TEE
2 sets of 8 reps

REPEAT Day 5 DRILL #2
REAR ELBOW GLOVE THROW
2 sets of 8 reps

Day 7 DRILL #1
REAR ARM UNDERHAND CATCH
3 sets of 8 reps
Get into a normal stance without a bat. Rest your front hand on your chest. Have a partner toss an underhand pitch to you from a close distance. Rotate your rear hip and catch the ball over the plate with your rear hand, palm facing up. Let the ball travel to you and do not reach for it. You may choose to use a tennis ball.

Day 7 DRILL #2
HIGH INSIDE REAR ARM PULL
3 sets of 8 reps
Using a choked-up grip with your rear arm only, hit off an inside high tee and pull the ball as much as possible. *Down 3rd for right hand hitters and down 1st for left-handed hitters. *Front shoulder is not opening!

Day 7 DRILL #3
FAST ATTACK FROM LOADED, STOP AT EXTENSION
3 sets of 8 reps
Get into a loaded and ready to hit position. As fast as possible, hit and finish through contact at extension before rollover. Finish at extension with barrel towards center field. Focus on getting on plane early and staying on plane with the pitch.

CATCH PHRASE: RELEASE
REMINDS TO: Feel the bat lag (slotted) position and achieve barrel release on the swing.

DAY 8: Keeping the Front Shoulder Closed

It is common to see highly athletic players struggle with hitting due to an issue with pulling the front shoulder. In my experience, this problem is often seen in players who have more powerful swings compared to their teammates. Excessive aggression in the swing can lead to swing flaws such as pulling off the ball, resulting in inconsistent contact with the ball. As coaches and parents, it is important not to suppress a player's aggression and power, but rather to teach them how to channel it effectively. It's about finding the balance between the player's natural power and the correct swing mechanics. It's important to focus on teaching the correct swing mechanics, while not taking away the player's natural power and aggression.

As with any isolation drill meant to correct some aspect of mechanics, we look for the counter-movement. The opposite of a front-side dominant swing flaw is creating rotation from the hitter's backside.

You will often see a hitter's back arm and elbow begin a move downward before their front shoulder begins rotating out. This squeeze of the back arm allows the shoulders to stay in line with the pitch while the core is beginning to rotate. This slotting move gets the bat into the zone early and allows it to stay through the hitting zone for the longest amount of time. This is what a short-to-long swing refers to.

A **Short to Long** swing in baseball refers to a swing technique where the hitter starts the swing with a shorter, more compact movement, and then extends or lengthens the swing as they contact the ball. This swing path allows the hitter to generate power and momentum while keeping their hands close to their body. It also allows the hitter to maintain control and make contact with a level swing path. The short to long swing path is often associated with more efficient use of the body's rotational forces and can be a very effective technique for generating power and increasing the chances of making solid contact with the ball.

Because barrel direction is improved, the ability for a hitter to impact the correct part of the ball at different depths across the plate increases.

Day 8 DRILL #1
SITTING BUCKET ONE ARM HIGH TEE
2 sets of 8 reps
Sitting on a bucket or something similar, set the tee up in a high position. Use the front arm only to hit the ball up the middle.
Use a one-hand trainer bat if available. Otherwise, use a choked-up grip.

Day 8 DRILL #2
STANDING ONE ARM HIGH TEE
2 sets of 8 reps
While standing set the tee up in a high position. Use the front arm only to hit the ball up the middle.
Use a one-hand trainer bat if available. Otherwise, use a choked-up grip.

Day 8 DRILL #3
BACK SIDE SINGLE HAND NET HOLD
3 sets of 5 reps
While standing, line up with your front foot against a batting net. Hold the net with your front hand. Use a choked-up single-hand grip with the rear hand. Rotate the rear shoulder and get aligned to the pitch and to contact without rotating the front shoulder.

Day 8 DRILL #4
CROSS TOSS OUTSIDE
3 sets of 8 reps
Using squishy baseballs or a safety screen, throw soft toss to the hitter from a close distance and at a 45-degree angle so that the pitch is crossing the

very outside of the plate. The hitter must hit a line drive to the opposite side of the field. I like doing this drill with Anywhere Baseballs and a half bat which are each linked in the products section.

Day 8 DRILL #5
SITTING BUCKET TWO HAND HIGH TEE

3 sets of 8 reps

Sitting on a bucket or something similar, set the tee up in a high position. With a normal grip on the bat, hit the ball up the middle.

DAY 9: Hand Path and Hands Inside the Ball

Hand path becomes a key element in a baseball swing once a player starts competitive travel ball or reaches middle school age and pitch velocity increases. A "laggy" or long swing will not be able to make contact since the "Time to Impact" will be too long.

Time to Impact in a baseball swing refers to the amount of time that elapses between the start of the swing and the moment of contact with the ball. This time frame is critical to the overall success of the swing, as it affects the hitter's ability to generate power and make accurate contact with the ball. A shorter time to impact allows for a faster swing and can lead to a harder hit, while a longer time to impact can result in a slower swing and a weaker hit. The ideal time to impact can vary depending on the player's swing style, but on average it's around .2 to .25 seconds. In general, a hitter needs to have a consistent and efficient swing, which will help them to generate power and make accurate contact with the ball.

Hands Inside the Ball is a reference to the hitter's hand path during a swing in relation to the baseball. The simplest way to translate this to a youth player is to sit a baseball on the front middle of the plate with the hitter in his stance and show that his hands stay inside of the path of the ball, rather than extending outward or away from the body. We covered the knob path extensively with our laser knob drills. This is considered to be an essential aspect of proper swing mechanics as it allows the hitter to generate a more compact and efficient swing, which leads to a greater chance of making solid contact with the ball.

Keeping the hands inside of the ball during a baseball swing can have a significant impact on time to impact. When the hands are positioned inside of the ball, the swing is shorter and more compact, allowing the hitter to make contact with the ball earlier in the swing. This results in a shorter time to impact, which can lead to a faster swing and harder hit.

Additionally, keeping the hands inside of the ball also allows the hitter to generate more power using the body's rotational forces. When the hands are inside of the ball, the barrel of the bat can travel on a flatter, more direct path to the ball, rather than looping around the outside of the ball. This direct path allows for a more efficient transfer of energy from the body to the bat, resulting in more power at the point of contact.

Furthermore, keeping the hands inside of the ball also allows the hitter to stay behind the ball longer and delay the rotation of the upper body, which can help to maintain a more level swing plane and improve accuracy. The longer the hitter stays behind the ball, the more time they have to make adjustments and track the pitch, which can lead to better pitch recognition and better contact.

Maintaining proper hand path during a swing is crucial for success at the plate and keeping the hands inside the ball is an essential aspect of this. The hand path can be difficult to discern without the aid of slow-motion video analysis or a trained eye.

There are two forces acting on the bat that generate bat speed: a circular hand path and torque applied at the handle. A circular hand path transfers body rotation into bat-head rotation. Better hitters keep their hands back and allow body rotation to accelerate their hands into a circular hand path. Average hitters use their arms to extend their hands toward the pitcher. The straighter the hand path, the less bat speed generated.

In summary, keeping the hands inside of the ball can lead to a shorter time to impact, more power, and improved accuracy. It's an essential aspect of proper swing mechanics and a key to generating consistent and hard contact with the ball.

Day 9 DRILL #1
KNOB TEE

3 sets of 8 reps

Set up a tee so that it is level with the hitter's chest. The hitter should stand with his/her front foot where the inside front corner of the plate would be. Use the bottom of the bat's knob to strike the ball.

CHECKPOINTS:

1. The knob should be making a u-turn motion to flatten out and strike the ball.
2. Barrel is snapping down and slotting
3. Front side is not pulling

REPEAT Day 8 DRILL #3
BACK SIDE SINGLE HAND NET HOLD
3 sets of 5 reps

REPEAT Day 2 DRILL #3
SIMULATED LASER KNOB TEE
2 sets of 5 reps

Day 9 DRILL #2
SWING INSIDE THE NET
2 sets of 5 reps
Place the bat on your belly button with the end of the bat about 1" away from a net. Swing without hitting the net. Be cautious of the hitter's front shoulder pulling out to make it easier, rather than truly keeping hands inside.

Day 9 DRILL #3
SWING INSIDE THE NET TEE
3 sets of 8 reps
Stay in the same position and use a tee. Enforce palm up/palm down at contact and back hand/arm pushing through.

Day 9 DRILL #4
DEEP OPPO TACO
3 sets of 8 reps
Set the tee up so that it is as deep and outside as possible. Focus on getting the barrel of the bat on plane with the pitch early in the swing, and drive the ball to the opposite field.

Day 9 DRILL #5
FRONT ARM FRISBEE
3 sets of 8 reps
From a normal batting stance, hold a frisbee with the bottom hand as if you are holding a bat. Perform a small load movement in the hand and pause for less than one second. Take a small step forward and land on the ball of the stride foot. Pause for less than one second and throw the frisbee toward center field. Freeze at extension with your index finger pointing towards center field.

For the last 2 sets of 8 reps, perform without any pauses, still finishing with index finger towards center field.

CHECKPOINTS:

1. If able, grip the frisbee with your index finger alongside the edge of it.
2. Load your hand back before throwing.
3. Finish with your index finger pointing towards center field.
4. Throwing hand should fall below the leading elbow during the throw.
5. Use your wrist to create spin on the frisbee.
6. Leading elbow should be used as a pivot point for the throwing hand
7. Like most drills, you are looking for mechanical accuracy, not power. ...yet.

CATCH PHRASE: SHORT TO LONG
REMINDS TO: Get the barrel into the strike zone with the shortest path and keep the barrel through the strike zone as long as possible.

DAYS 10-13 : CONTACT AND FINISHING THE SWING

DAY 10: Contact Position and Bat Vertical Angle at Impact

The goal here is to really get a feel for how the bag gets lagged on the rear shoulder, the rear elbow is on the rear hip, and the rear hand is pushing through. A swing with bat drag does not achieve this position since the hitter more than likely will be unable to achieve a palm up/palm down position at contact. Stay focused on the front shoulder not pulling out and emphasize keeping the chest/upper half from rotating before the bottom half starts to rotate. The hitter MUST be able to achieve separation of the top and bottom half.

Bat Vertical Angle at Impact: This measure is the bat's degrees relative to zero in relation to the knob of the bat when contact is made. A negative measure is indicative of the barrel being below the hands at contact, which is what we want. A target measure is around -25 to -35 degrees.

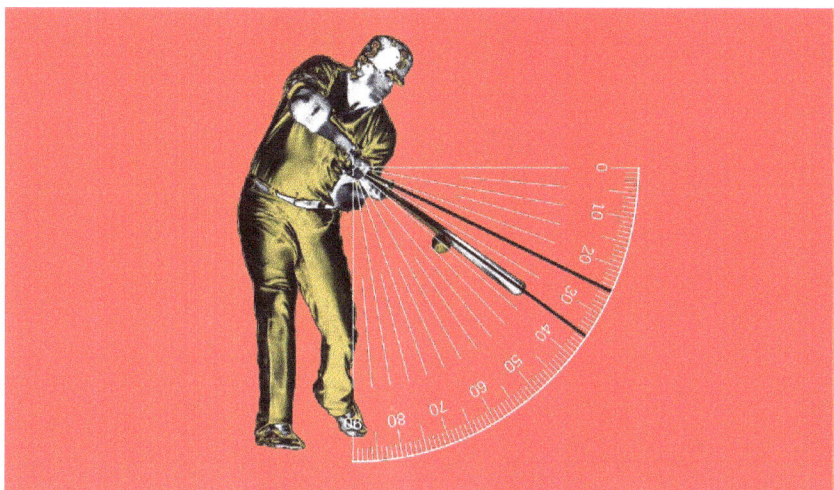

BAT VERTICAL ANGLE AT IMPACT -25 TO -35 DEGREES

To add some insight and application to this data, realize that it is important that the hitter can control the knob of the bat. Understand that it is important to ensure that the hitter has the wrist and forearm strength to control the size of the bat being used. This is where balanced vs end-loaded bats come into play. It is okay to be a player that uses either. It's even better if you are using what matches the type of hitter that you are. Most should use a balanced or less end-loaded bat. If you are an ox that hits nukes, you are probably going to prefer end-loaded.

You should see the barrel drop slightly below the hands when moving from bat lag to contact position. The keyword is "slightly". Wherever contact is made, the hands should be above the baseball and the barrel below the hands. No swords!

STAYING BEHIND THE BALL

In the above image, we can see the example of proper technique in a baseball swing demonstrated by a professional. One of the key elements to note is how he maintains his position behind the ball at the point of contact.

Staying Behind the Ball refers to the position of the hands, barrel, and body in relation to the ball as it travels towards the plate. This typically involves maintaining a slight bend in the knees and keeping the weight back and over the back leg, rather than lunging forward too early. This is considered an ideal position for a powerful and accurate swing, and it is important to focus on replicating this movement during practice and training.

Notice the vertical alignment of the head, back hip, and back knee, as well as the underhand punch motion of the rear arm. Additionally, the rear knee is positioned in front of the buttocks at the moment of contact, with the rear foot on the tip of his toes.

This is further accentuated by the locked-out front leg and closed front foot, which together forms the axis of rotation for the swing. All these elements work together to create a swing that is both powerful and precise.

REPEAT Day 2 DRILL #3
SIMULATED LASER KNOB TEE
2 sets of 5 reps

REPEAT Day 9 DRILL #1
KNOB TEE
2 sets of 8 reps

REPEAT Day 8 DRILL #3
BACK SIDE SINGLE HAND NET HOLD
2 sets of 8 reps

DAY 10 DRILL #1
FOUR POINT CHECK (LOAD, STRIDE, SLOT, CONTACT) TEE
3 sets of 8 reps
The hitter or coach should say each of the steps out loud: "Load, Stride, Slot, Contact". Pause briefly at each step and hold the contact position for one second. Reset and take a normal swing off a tee to complete one rep. Like many drills, you are looking for mechanical accuracy, not power. Use 75% power swings and focus on the mechanics.

CHECKPOINTS:

1. Short hand path to the ball
2. Hands path stays inside of the ball
3. Hands are palm up / palm down at contact
4. Bat Vertical Angle at Impact is -25 to -35 degrees
5. Stride foot is landing softly on the ball of the foot
6. Front Heel Plant occurs before moving into the slot position
7. Maintain Dynamic Balance

REPEAT Day 7 DRILL #3
FAST ATTACK FROM LOADED, STOP AT EXTENSION
3 sets of 5 reps

REPEAT Day 9 DRILL #4
DEEP OPPO TACO
3 sets of 5 reps

DAY 11: Load & Stride, Slot, Contact Build the Muscle Memory

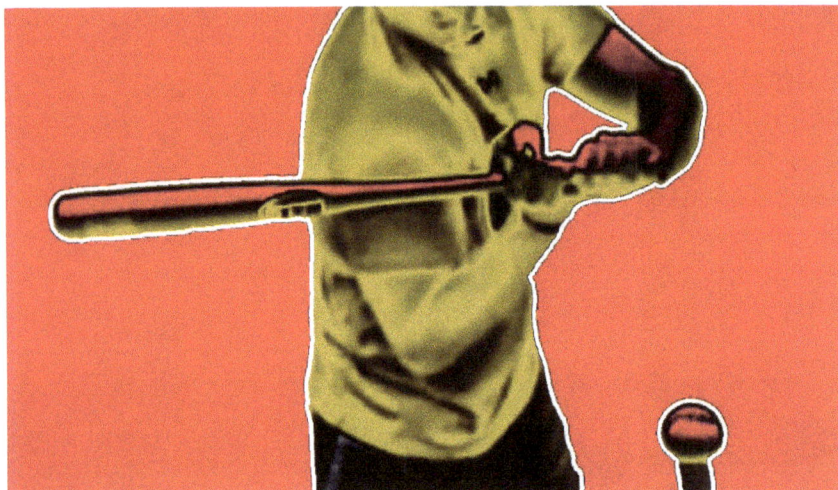

To consistently hit with power, it is essential to practice and build fluidity in the steps of your swing. Repeatedly practicing the proper technique will help to develop the muscle memory and timing needed to execute a powerful swing. An important aspect of this technique is the sequence of load & stride, slot (bat lag), and contact.

As a reminder, the slot and bat lag position refers to the position of the bat that is shown in the above image. When loaded, the knob of the bat is facing toward the catcher. When lagged, the knob is facing toward the pitcher.

To maintain good form, the barrel of the bat should stay close to the rear shoulder and fall below the hands as the swing progresses. This occurs when the barrel is released from the lagged position to contact the ball. It's crucial for the player to know what it feels like to release the barrel and feel the right timing. By focusing on proper technique and building fluidity through repetition, players can achieve consistent contact and power in their swings.

With that said, **I am a believer in the LINE DRIVE PRO. BUY IT, USE IT!**

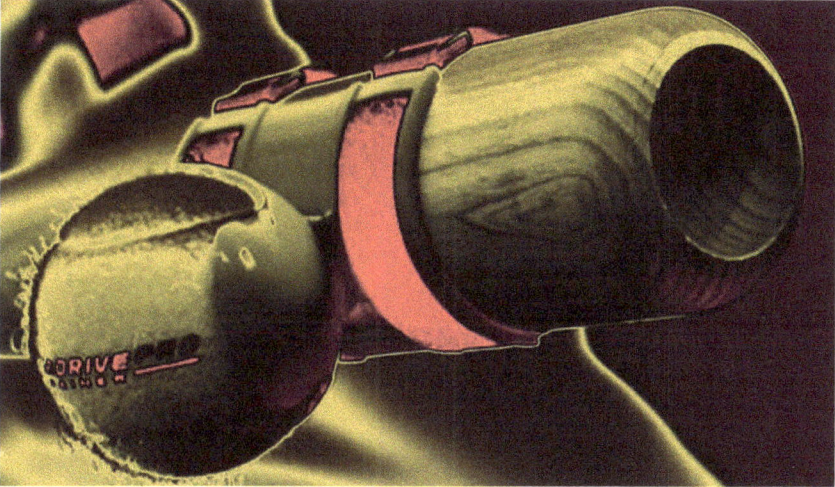

LINE DRIVE PRO
https://baseballhittingaid.com

My 12-year-old son (8 at the time) had been experiencing a problem with pulling his front shoulder during his swing. We revisited this tool to address the issue and as always, there was an immediate improvement. However, it's important to note that using this tool alone won't instantly fix the problem. Consistent training and repetition, along with proper coaching and explanation, are crucial to see the desired results. The progress comes with some initial frustration and requires repetition and coaching to see the desired results. This is an effective drill that provides instant feedback and allows for quick correction, making it a valuable tool in the player's training. I find it to be quite fun.

REPEAT Day 7 DRILL #1
REAR ARM UNDERHAND CATCH
3 sets of 8 reps

REPEAT Day 5 DRILL #2
REAR ELBOW GLOVE THROW
3 sets of 5 reps

Day 11 DRILL #1
LOAD & STRIDE, SLOT, HIT
3 sets of 8 reps
From a normal batting stance, load & stride and pause for 1 second, slot and pause for one second, then hit the ball off the tee to complete one rep.

REPEAT Day 7 DRILL #3
FAST ATTACK FROM LOADED, STOP AT EXTENSION
3 sets of 8 reps

REPEAT Day 6 DRILL #2
THE GRIFFEY
3 sets of 8 reps

Day 11 DRILL #2
FRONT TOSS FAKE OUT
3 sets of 8 reps
Take normal swings with a partner tossing an underhand front toss at a short distance behind a safety screen. The partner should randomly hold onto the ball at the point where it would have been released toward the batter. On this fake-out throw, check that the hitter maintains a good ready-to-hit launch position and has not yet performed Front Heel Plant. This drill is great for working with players who need help with tracking, timing, and hitting off-speed pitches.

Day 11 DRILL #3
LINE DRIVE PRO
3 sets of 8 reps
If you DO NOT have the Line Drive Pro, find an old bat, and have the hitter swing and throw the bat toward second base at least a few times.

DAY 12: Extension & Follow Through

<u>Extension</u> in a baseball swing refers to the full extension of the body and the arms through the point of contact with the ball. It is the final moment after contact where the player's arms, shoulders, hips, and legs are fully extended, creating a straight line from the back foot to the hands. This full extension allows the player to generate maximum power and speed in the swing, resulting in a harder hit and potentially longer distance. This position should be familiar as there were previous drills where the swing stopped at extension.

Proper extension also allows the player to maintain good form and balance throughout the swing, enabling them to make contact with the ball in the correct spot on the bat, which in turn will help to hit the ball with accuracy. As you can see in the image above, the hitter has achieved full extension in his swing. His arms, shoulders, hips, and legs are fully extended, with his rear knee, hands, and barrel pointing toward center field. Notice that the wrists have not yet rolled over. This is an ideal position that allows the hitter to generate maximum power.

The **Follow Through** in a baseball swing refers to the final step of the swing and occurs after contact and extension. It is the continuation motion of the swing where the wrists roll over as the hands and barrel continue to travel around the body.

A good follow-through is crucial for the player to maintain good form and balance at this stage. Proper follow-through can add more power, increase bat speed, and improve overall consistency. It also helps to transfer the energy from the body to the bat, which in turn impacts the ball's trajectory, distance, and exit velocity. The follow-through is used to help the hitter maintain balance and control, allowing them to stay in the correct position to complete the swing.

REPEAT Day 9 DRILL #5
FRONT ARM FRISBEE
2 sets of 8 reps

Day 12 DRILL #1
TOP HAND UPSIDE-DOWN
3 sets of 8 reps

From a normal batting stance, flip the top hand upside down, positioning it close to the top of the grip. Take swings while finishing with an extended reach toward center field. This grip allows players to experience the sensation of turning the barrel as opposed to pushing it. It also helps players understand the feeling of a loaded rear shoulder and can correct the habit of casting the hands away from the body. The upside-down top hand grip promotes keeping the hands and barrel closer to the body, creates a shorter path to the ball, and encourages proper extension through contact.

REPEAT Day 10 DRILL #2
TEE WITH FOUR POINT CHECK (LOAD, STRIDE, SLOT, HIT TO EXTENSION)
3 sets of 5 reps

Day 12 DRILL #2
FLAT PALM TOP HAND
3 sets of 8 reps

From a normal batting stance, take the top hand and open it up, so it is in a high-five position. Place the flat hand behind the handle of the bat, with the palm facing across into the other batter's box. Take swings while focusing on keeping the top hand flat and behind the handle, pushing the bat through contact and finishing with arms extended towards center field. This drill too helps players understand the sensation of turning the barrel instead of pushing it and promotes a shorter path to the ball.

REPEAT DAY 8 DRILL #4
CROSS TOSS OUTSIDE
3 sets of 8 reps

Day 12 DRILL #3
SWING TO CONTACT, RESET AND HOLD FINISH
3 sets of 8 reps

From a normal stance, load and simulate a live swing but stop just before contacting the ball. Hold the bat at contact position 1 second. Reset and take a full swing and freeze at the end of your swing, keeping your eyes at contact.

CHECKPOINTS FOR CONTACT POSITION:

1. Bat Vertical Angle at Impact - barrel is slightly below the hands
2. Grip on the bat is near palm up / palm down
3. Stay Behind the Ball - Contact with the ball is occurring if front of the hitter's front leg

CHECKPOINTS FOR FINISH POSITION:

1. Chin from shoulder to shoulder, eyes stay at contact
2. Finish over top of front shoulder
3. Rear shoulder over the plate
4. Stay Behind the Ball

CATCH PHRASE: LIFT IT
REMINDS TO: Continue pushing through contact without rolling the wrists over. Feel extension towards center field and finish over the front shoulder.

DAY 13: Bringing It All Together

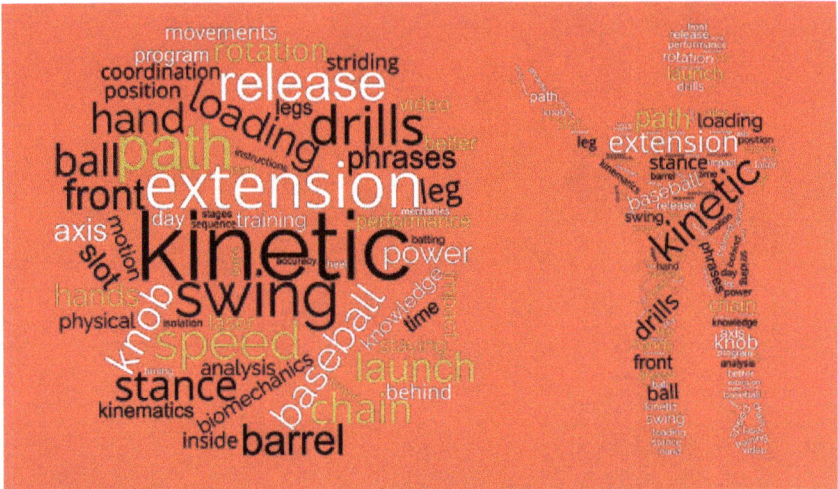

A wide range of topics related to baseball swing mechanics have been discussed, including the kinetic chain, the stages of a swing, proper grip and alignment, hand and leg loading, bat lag and barrel release, proper contact position, and follow-through. Additionally, specific drills and techniques for improving swing mechanics were discussed.

Tips for coaching and teaching swing mechanics were discussed, including the use of catch phrases to communicate effectively with players. You should now have a deep understanding of the mechanics of a baseball swing and various strategies for improving and teaching swing mechanics.

A player who has absorbed all the information covered in this program should have a solid foundation in the mechanics of a baseball swing, as well as the ability to identify and address specific areas that need improvement.

Day 13 DRILL #1
QUIZ ON CATCH PHRASES AND CHECKPOINTS
Quiz the player on catch phrases, what they mean, and all checkpoints.

Day 13 DRILL #2
FINISH LINE
Perform 5 reps of every drill starting at Day 1.

Congratulations on completing the 13 Day Better Baseball Swing training program!

The program is designed to teach about the kinetic chain in a baseball swing, which is a crucial aspect of hitting a baseball. By learning about the kinetic chain, you have gained a deeper understanding of how the body works together to generate power, bat speed, and accuracy in your swing.

It's not an easy task to complete a training program, and the fact that you have done it demonstrates your commitment and determination to improve your skills. The 13 Day Better Baseball Swing training program has provided you with the tools and knowledge to take your game or coaching to the next level.

The kinetic chain is a complex concept, but by understanding it, you have unlocked the potential to become more powerful and accurate whether you are a player or a coach. Keep applying the concepts you've learned and continue to practice, and you'll see even more improvement in your swing or in your players' swings.

The dedication and hard work you put into the program will pay off, and you should be proud of your accomplishment. The 13 days of training has helped you to develop a more efficient and effective swing or coaching technique, which will surely improve your performance on the field.

Keep practicing and using the knowledge and skills you've gained from the program, and you'll continue to see improvements in your game. Great Work!

All Drills and Instructions

Day 1 DRILL #1
GRIP, STANCE, AND LOAD REVIEW
Review the CHECKPOINTS and quiz the player on positioning.

CHECKPOINTS:

1. Stance (Pre-Load)
    a. Toes point straight ahead (can be more closed)
    b. Stance is slightly open, rear foot is slightly closer to the plate
    c. Knees are BENT, no straight or stiff legs
    d. Feet are wider than shoulders
    e. Hands in front of rear shoulder
    f. Bat is over the shoulder at nearly a 45-degree angle
    g. Bat is behind the helmet
    h. Top half is slightly over the plate, not straight up and down

2. Load
    a. Weight of the back foot is on the inside, NOT outside, of the rear foot and is ready to launch towards the pitched ball.
    b. Front shoulder is slightly rolled with both eyes able to see the pitcher. Don't roll your front shoulder too much as you load and take away your rear eye from seeing the ball.
    c. Knees and hips pinch together - almost as if a ball is being squeezed between the knees. ("Closed hips")
    d. Back knee and front knee stay bent throughout load

Day 1 DRILL #2
GRIP, STANCE, AND LOAD CHECKPOINTS
3 sets of 5 reps
Get into a proper stance and say load. Say each of the checkpoints out loud while loaded and hit a ball off a tee from this position. When performing tee drills, make sure that contact is occurring in front of the front leg

CHECKPOINTS:

1. Knees bent
2. Weight on inside of back foot
3. Hands back, in front of shoulder
4. Knob at catcher
5. Grip *(Stick index fingers out, should point upwards)*
6. Both eyes on pitcher

Day 2 DRILL #1
REAR SHOULDER PINCH
3 sets of 5 reps

Perform the first set of 5 reps without a bat, using a two-hand grip on your invisible bat. From a normal resting stance, slightly roll the rear shoulder inwards as if you are pouring out a coffee mug towards your chest. This moves the hands back and points the knob at the catcher. This is a SMALL movement. Control the path of the knob. The position should be very similar to your position if you were preparing to throw a strong punch.

CHECKPOINTS:

1. Toes pointed straight ahead, and knees are bent
2. Position of the handsPosition of the hands:
   a. Hands are in front of rear shoulder from a side view
   b. Hands are in front of toe line from top-down view
   c. Wrists are angled, not flat with the forearms.
   d. **We are NOT pushing the hands back**
3. Knob of bat points at or near catcher's glove
4. Hitter is hiding hands from the pitcher
5. **Slight** stretch in leading arm deltoid and lat muscles but NOT barring out the arm

Day 2 DRILL #2
LASER KNOB
3 sets of 5 reps

Rig up a laser pointer or flashlight to the bottom of the bat handle with some tape. Get into a normal stance with the laser pointed towards the ground near the back of the plate. Load slowly and move the laser dot in a straight line away from the back tip of the plate. Once in the loaded position with the laser pointed towards the catcher, move the laser dot back up the straight line that you first made using your wrists only as much as possible and keeping your hands back near the rear shoulder. Once the straight line of the laser dot gets well past the front of the plate, snap to contact position.

Day 2 DRILL #3
SIMULATED LASER KNOB TEE
3 sets of 8 reps

Remove the laser pointer and perform the same action with a simulated laser pointer on the end of your knob. Load slowly and move the simulated laser dot in a straight line away from the back tip of the plate. Once in the loaded position with the laser pointed towards the catcher, move the laser dot back up the straight line that you first made using only your wrists as much as possible. Once the straight line of the simulated laser dot gets well past the front of the plate, hit the ball off the tee and finish with both arms extended, pointing towards center field.

Day 3 DRILL #1
LOAD CHECK STRIDE CHECK HIT
3 sets of 8 reps

Load, check hands, stride, check hands. Say each out loud or in your head during the movements. Briefly pause at each step. Reset and hit one ball off the tee without pausing at each step to complete one rep.

CHECKPOINTS:

1. Hands and top half are the same when loaded and after the stride
2. Feet are about one bat length apart
3. Front knee slightly bent after stride
4. Front shoulder stays slightly lower than rear shoulder
5. From side view, core and upper half stays vertically straight
6. Stride foot is at 30-45 degree when landing
7. Elbows stay separated throughout stance, load, and hip explosion.
8. Core / Belly Button does not travel forwards towards the pitcher

Day 3 DRILL #2
TWO STEP WALK UP
3 sets of 8 reps

Stand Behind the batter's box with your chest facing the pitcher. Take two steps forward, stride foot first and plant your rear foot into the batter's box on the second step. Have the rear foot turned and facing in the correct direction when it lands. Continue into your stride to hit the ball off the tee. Feel the separation being created between your stride foot and your hands. Feel how your core wants to coil up as you rotate your body into the hitting position.

Day 4 DRILL #1
FRONT FOOT BALL STEP CHECK
2 sets of 5 reps

Place a medicine ball, or basketball, under the front foot while in a batting stance. Feel the activation in the quad, hamstring, and heel. Feel how stable you are. Raise the front foot off the top of the ball and slowly step over it towards the pitcher. Land in a ready-to-hit position on the ball of the front foot. Remember that we are not yet planting the front heel. That will occur with hip rotation.

Day 4 DRILL #2
FRONT FOOT BALL STEP TEE
2 sets of 8 reps
Place a medicine ball, or basketball, under the front foot while in a batting stance. Feel the activation in the quad, hamstring, and heel. Raise the front foot off the top of the ball and step over it towards the pitcher, hitting the ball off the tee. Use the half bat and 'anywhere balls' if available.

Day 4 DRILL #3
STRIDE BOX
3 sets of 8 reps
To perform this drill, a small flat box or a square of tape is placed on the ground in front of the batter, representing the ideal stride position. The batter should take their normal stance and focus on striding into the box and keeping dynamic balance. The batter should make sure that their front foot lands within the box or tape and that their weight is distributed evenly between both legs. We are taking a small step and landing softly on the ball of the front foot with a bent knee.

After the first set of 8 reps, or once the batter is comfortable with striding into the box, they can progress to taking swings while focusing on maintaining their launch position. The coach or partner can observe the batter and give feedback on any adjustments that need to be made.

Day 5 DRILL #1
STANCE, LOAD, STRIDE, HIP SEQUENCE CHECK
2 sets of 5 reps
Say each step out loud, or in your head, while moving to each position. Pause in between and check each position. We are NOT moving the hands forward or getting into the slot position. On the word hip, you are opening the hips and rotating your bottom half to feel the separation and stretch in your front deltoid and lat while keeping your hands back. Start to flatten out the bat by turning the knob towards the pitcher on the word hips. Feel the connection between firing your hips and firing your hands. Feel how you can adjust the timing between your hips and hands to create either a short contact swing or a loaded-up power swing.

Day 5 DRILL #2
REAR ELBOW GLOVE THROW
3 sets of 8 reps
Tuck a glove or deflated ball in-between the rear elbow and the hip. Throw it in front of the plate when hitting the ball off a tee. You are not hitting with power, just focusing on the direction of the glove throw up the middle.

Day 5 DRILL #3
BAT LAG TO EXTENSION TEE
3 sets of 8 reps
Start at Bat lag (slotted) position with the rear elbow on the hip and the knob towards the pitcher. The barrel of the bat should be near the rear arm. Hit off the tee and finish in the extension position without rolling the wrists over. The end of the barrel should point towards center field.

Day 5 DRILL #4
BAT LAG TO EXTENSION FRONT TOSS
3 sets of 8 reps
Repeat with front soft toss. 3 sets of 8 reps. Start at Bat lag (slotted) elbow on hip position. Hit and finish in extension position without rolling the wrists over.

Day 6 DRILL #1
HIP EXPLOSION ISOLATION
2 sets of 8 reps
From the loaded position, take a small stride step. When the front heel touches down, explosively rotate the back knee towards the front leg as fast as possible to trigger hip rotation. Enforce the hitter shifting the loaded weight forward towards the pitcher. This movement should cause the rear heel to raise, and even better if we can simulate some rear foot toe drag. The hands and knob should be firing the into the slot position immediately after the hips

Day 6 DRILL #2
THE GRIFFEY
3 sets of 8 reps
Get into your batting stance with your feet almost all the way together. Make sure to relax your hands. When taking a step forward, you should naturally create separation between your stride food and hands. When your stride foot lands, make sure that you are in a good ready-to-hit launch position. You want to feel nice and relaxed and use the planting of the stride foot heel as a timing mechanism to fire the hips and start the swing.

Day 6 DRILL #3
REAR KNEE FOLLOW THROUGH

3 sets of 8 reps

From a normal stance and with normal timing, hit a ball off the tee and finish with your rear knee continuing forward and upward. Feel the axis or rotation on a stiffened front leg. Feel opposing rotation in the front side of your body, meaning that you can feel your front leg and front of your core resist the backside rotation from the rear knee and hips. This stabilizes the batter and helps to maintain dynamic balance (head over sternum over belly button).

Day 6 DRILL #4
REAR NET

3 sets of 8 reps

Get into a batting stance with your rear foot about 4-6 inches away from a net or fence behind you. Stride away from the rear net/fence to hit the ball off a tee. The player should be able to swing without hitting the rear net/fence.

Day 7 DRILL #1
REAR ARM UNDERHAND CATCH

3 sets of 8 reps

Get into a normal stance without a bat. Rest your front hand on your chest. Have a partner toss an underhand pitch to you from a close distance. Rotate your rear hip and catch the ball with your rear hand, palm facing up. Let the ball travel to you and do not reach for it. You may choose to use a tennis ball.

Day 7 DRILL #2
HIGH INSIDE REAR ARM PULL

3 sets of 8 reps

Using a choked-up grip with your rear arm only, hit off an inside high tee and pull the ball as much as possible. *Down 3rd for right hand hitters and down 1st for left-handed hitters. *Front shoulder is not opening!

Day 7 DRILL #3
FAST ATTACK FROM LOADED, STOP AT EXTENSION

3 sets of 8 reps

Get into a loaded and ready-to-hit position. As fast as possible, hit and finish through contact at extension before rollover. Finish at extension with barrel towards center field. Focus on getting on plane early and staying on plane with the pitch.

Day 8 DRILL #1
SITTING BUCKET ONE ARM HIGH TEE
2 sets of 8 reps
Sitting on a bucket or something similar, set the tee up in a high position.
Use the front arm only to hit the ball up the middle.
Use a one-hand trainer bat if available. Otherwise, use a choked-up grip.

Day 8 DRILL #2
STANDING ONE ARM HIGH TEE
2 sets of 8 reps
While standing, set the tee up in a high position. Use the front arm only to
hit the ball up the middle.
Use a one-hand trainer bat if available. Otherwise, use a choked-up grip.

Day 8 DRILL #3
BACK SIDE SINGLE HAND NET HOLD
3 sets of 5 reps
While standing, line up with your front foot against a batting net. Hold the
net with your front hand. Use a choked up single hand grip with the rear
hand. Rotate the rear shoulder and get aligned to the pitch and to contact
without rotating the front shoulder.

Day 8 DRILL #4
CROSS TOSS OUTSIDE
3 sets of 8 reps
Using squishy baseballs or a safety screen, throw soft toss to the hitter from
a close distance and at a 45-degree angle so that the pitch is crossing the
very outside of the plate. The hitter must hit a line drive to the opposite
side of the field. I like doing this drill with Anywhere Baseballs and a half
bat which are each linked in the products section.

Day 8 DRILL #5
SITTING BUCKET TWO HAND HIGH TEE
3 sets of 8 reps
Sitting on a bucket or something similar, set the tee up in a high position.
With a normal grip on the bat, hit the ball up the middle.

Day 9 DRILL #1
KNOB TEE
3 sets of 8 reps
Set up a tee so that it is level with the hitter's chest. The hitter should stand
with his/her front foot where the inside front corner of the plate would be.
Use the bottom of the bat's knob to strike the ball.

CHECKPOINTS:

1. The knob should be making a u-turn motion to flatten out and strike the ball.
2. Barrel is snapping down and slotting
3. Front side is not pulling

Day 9 DRILL #2
SWING INSIDE THE NET
2 sets of 5 reps
Place the bat on your belly button with the end of the bat about 1" away from a net. Swing without hitting the net. Be cautious of the hitter's front shoulder pulling out to make it easier, rather than truly keeping hands inside.

Day 9 DRILL #3
SWING INSIDE THE NET TEE
3 sets of 8 reps
Stay in the same position and use a tee. Enforce palm up/palm down at contact and back hand/arm pushing through.

Day 9 DRILL #4
DEEP OPPO TACO
3 sets of 8 reps
Set the tee up so that it is as deep and outside as possible. Focus on getting the barrel of the bat on plane with the pitch early in the swing, and drive the ball to the opposite field.

Day 9 DRILL #5
FRONT ARM FRISBEE
3 sets of 8 reps
From a normal batting stance, hold a frisbee with the bottom hand as if you are holding a bat. Perform a small load movement in the hand and pause for less than one second. Take a small step forward and land on the ball of the stride foot. Pause for less than one second and throw the frisbee towards center field. Freeze at extension with your index finger pointing towards center field.

For the last 2 sets of 8 reps, perform without any pauses, still finishing with index finger towards center field.

CHECKPOINTS:

1. If able, grip the frisbee with your index finger alongside the edge of it.

2. Load your hand back before throwing.
3. Finish with your index finger pointing towards center field.
4. Throwing hand should fall below the leading elbow during the throw.
5. Use your wrist to create spin on the frisbee.
6. Leading elbow should be used as a pivot point for the throwing hand
7. Like most drills, you are looking for mechanical accuracy, not power. …yet.

DAY 10 DRILL #1
FOUR POINT CHECK (LOAD, STRIDE, SLOT, CONTACT) TEE
3 sets of 8 reps

The hitter or coach should say each of the steps out loud: "Load, Stride, Slot, Contact". Pause briefly at each step and hold the contact position for one second. Reset and take a normal swing off a tee to complete one rep. Like many drills, you are looking for mechanical accuracy, not power. Use 75% power swings and focus on the mechanics.

CHECKPOINTS:

1. Short hand path to the ball
2. Hands path stays inside of the ball
3. Hands are palm up / palm down at contact
4. Bat Vertical Angle at Impact is -25 to -35 degrees
5. Stride foot is landing softly on the ball of the foot
6. Front Heel Plant occurs before moving into the slot position
7. Maintain Dynamic Balance

Day 11 DRILL #1
LOAD & STRIDE, SLOT, HIT
3 sets of 8 reps

From a normal batting stance, load & stride and pause for 1 second, slot and pause for one second, then hit the ball off the tee to complete one rep.

Day 11 DRILL #2
FRONT TOSS FAKE OUT
3 sets of 8 reps

Take normal swings with a partner tossing an underhand front toss at a short distance behind a safety screen. The partner should randomly hold onto the ball at the point where it would have been released towards the batter. On this fake out throw, check that the hitter maintains a good ready-to-hit launch position and has not yet performed Front Heel Plant. This drill is great for working with players who need help with tracking, timing, and hitting off-speed pitches.

Day 11 DRILL #3
LINE DRIVE PRO
3 sets of 8 reps
If you DO NOT have the Line Drive Pro, find an old bat, and have the hitter swing and throw the bat towards second base at least a few times.

Day 12 DRILL #1
TOP HAND UPSIDE-DOWN
3 sets of 8 reps
From a normal batting stance, flip the top hand upside down, positioning it close to the top of the grip. Take swings while finishing with an extended reach towards center field. This grip allows players to experience the sensation of turning the barrel as opposed to pushing it. It also helps players understand the feeling of a loaded rear shoulder and can correct the habit of casting the hands away from the body. The upside-down top hand grip promotes keeping the hands and barrel closer to the body, creates a shorter path to the ball, and encourages proper extension through contact.

Day 12 DRILL #2
FLAT PALM TOP HAND
3 sets of 8 reps
From a normal batting stance, take the top hand and open it up, so it is in a high-five position. Place the flat hand behind the handle of the bat, with the palm facing across into the other batter's box. Take swings while focusing on keeping the top hand flat and behind the handle, pushing the bat through contact and finishing with arms extended towards center field. This drill too helps players understand the sensation of turning the barrel instead of pushing it and promotes a shorter path to the ball.

Day 12 DRILL #3
SWING TO CONTACT, RESET AND HOLD FINISH
3 sets of 8 reps
From a normal stance, load and simulate a live swing but stop just before contacting the ball. Hold the bat at contact position 1 second. Reset and take a full swing and freeze at the end of your swing, keeping your eyes at contact.

CHECKPOINTS FOR CONTACT POSITION:

1. Bat Vertical Angle at Impact - barrel is slightly below the hands
2. Grip on the bat is near palm up / palm down

3. Stay Behind the Ball - Contact with the ball is occurring if front of the hitter's front leg

CHECKPOINTS FOR FINISH POSITION:

1. Chin from shoulder to shoulder, eyes stay at contact
2. Finish over top of front shoulder
3. Rear shoulder over the plate
4. Stay Behind the Ball

Day 13 DRILL #1
QUIZ ON CATCH PHRASES AND CHECKPOINTS
Quiz the player on catch phrases, what they mean, and all checkpoints.

Day 13 DRILL #2
FINISH LINE
Perform 5 reps of every drill starting at Day 1.

REFERENCE

The Biomechanics of the Baseball Swing - University of Miami
https://scholarlyrepository.miami.edu/cgi/viewcontent.cgi?article=1550&context=oa_dissertations

Bat Sizing Chart

Player	Recommended Bat Weight (oz)
Major League Baseball	Height/3 + 7
Amateur Baseball	Height/3 + 6
Fastpitch Softball	Height/7 + 20
Slow Pitch Softball	Weight/115 + 24
Junior League Baseball (13-17 yrs.)	Height/3 + 1
Little League Baseball (11-12 yrs.)	Weight/18 + 16
Little League Baseball (9-10 yrs.)	Height/3 + 4
Little League Baseball (7-8 yrs.)	Age*2 + 4

Training Tools

Home Depot Axe Handle
Good for slotting and palm up, palm down work; also helps with learning to 'turn the barrel'.
https://www.homedepot.com/p/True-Temper-36-in-Axe-Replacement-Handle-2036700/100605578
My 12 year old son using this:
https://www.youtube.com/shorts/i4HGec6SMNE

Rope Bat
Helps create bat speed and teaches to feel the whip effect in a swing by utilizing centrifugal force
https://ropebat.com/

Line Drive Pro
Good for barrel release timing and launch angle. Spotlights swing flaws like casting the hands.
https://baseballhittingaid.com/
https://ugoprobaseball.com/product/linedrivepro-swing-trainer-bundle/

One Hand Trainer Baseball Bat
18" for youth, 22" for 13 yrs old and up. There are many to choose from. One example is:
https://www.amazon.com/Axe-One-Hand-Trainer-Baseball-1-Piece/dp/B08R6DC78N/

Half Bat
Learn how to 'turn the barrel' instead of 'pushing the barrel'
https://www.halfbat.com/collections/all

The Anywhere Baseball
Soft foam baseballs for use with a half bat or training "anywhere".
Good for cross toss.
https://www.amazon.com/gp/product/B00GWYK28I

Weighted Baseballs
I've used these for several teams and have thousands of hits on them
without any issues.
https://www.amazon.com/Rukket-Weighted-Baseballs-Softballs-
Pitching/dp/B01HBPL78K/

An effective way to enforce extension and follow through is to hit weighted
balls. The younger the player, the closer and slower the toss.

Tanner Tee
Batting tee with rolled rubber top.
https://www.tannertees.com/tanner-tee-the-original/

Media Links

Lucas (Class of 2024)
https://twitter.com/LucasBolin2024

2022 - 15/16 yrs. old
Sophomore playing Varsity
https://www.youtube.com/watch?v=fxOT8ATgl8Q

2022 High School. Stats
https://scoreboard.12dt.com/scoreboard/khsaa/kyba22/?id=stats_87110_0

—-----------------------------------

Brooks (Class of 2028)
https://twitter.com/Brooks2028

2018 - 7 to 8 yrs. Old Batting Development
https://www.youtube.com/watch?v=RFX3j3U1D_8

2018 - 7 to 8 yrs. Old Batting Highlights and Homeruns
https://www.youtube.com/watch?v=m5LDycQJzzs&t=16s

2019 - 9 yrs. old
USSSA Kentucky 10U All-State Home Run Derby Champ
https://www.youtube.com/watch?v=2ayDTiTbGuI&t=84s

2022 - 12-Year-Old Homerun 250+ft
https://www.youtube.com/watch?v=2LGLdmpqo6Y

2022 - 12-Year-Old Homerun 270ft
USSSA Kentucky 11/12U All-State Showcase
https://www.youtube.com/watch?v=aPMKMmznfyY

2022 Highlights.
https://www.youtube.com/watch?v=sVkxPj29hs4

Sign up for the newsletter.

Sign up to receive my hitting tips newsletter
and you'll be automatically entered to win
FREE baseball training products.

*Winners will be notified via email
and announced on social media.

Start your journey to a better swing today!

https://betterbaseballswing.com

www.ingramcontent.com/pod-product-compliance
Lightning Source LLC
Chambersburg PA
CBHW071840090426

42737CB00031B/2469